COURAGE

Written & Compiled by Amelia Riedler
Designed by Emily Carlson

MY WILL SHALL SHAPE MY FUTURE... MY CHOICE; MY RESPONSIBILITY; WIN OR LOSE, ONLY I HOLD THE KEY TO MY DESTINY.

Elaine Maxwell

The world is large, and there can be many dark places full of challenges, and obstacles, and setbacks to overcome. But with courage, we offer ourselves a choice, and a light to get us through.

It doesn't take much: a single thought, a single word, a single spark—and our world ignites. Because courage is about moving forward in spite of fears and doubts. It's about accepting what your heart is telling you. And it's about taking a risk, even when you don't know what will come next.

So shine a light on the shadows, and reveal what you need to see. It will be hard. But it will be amazing. And it will be beautiful. There is no easy path, but there is a worthwhile one. And if you really look, you will find the courage you need. It will be there, with each and every act of bravery you take.

ONE STEP
CAN BE
need. ⇒

forward
ALL YOU

$\longrightarrow$

ONE STEP
CAN CHANGE
EVERY

FORWARD THINKING.

SOMETIMES THE BIGGEST ACT OF COURAGE IS A SMALL ONE.

Lauren Raffo

EVERY

IN YOUR life

YOU FOR

THING HAS prepared THIS.

YOU HAVE

everyt

hing

IT TAKES.

YOU WERE
GIVEN THIS LIFE
BECAUSE YOU
WERE STRONG
ENOUGH
TO LIVE IT.

Unknown

BEING brave
WITHOUT FEAR
IS CHOOSI
matters

ISN'T BEING
BEING
BEING BRAVE
NG what
MOST.

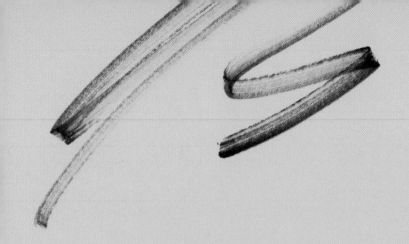

NEVER HAV

FOLLOW YO

Un

E REGRETS,

UR HEART.

n

BE AFRAID OF
NOTHING. YOU HAVE
WITHIN YOU ALL
WISDOM, ALL POWER,
ALL STRENGTH, ALL
UNDERSTANDING.

Eileen Caddy

no one

AWAY YO

your DETE

CAN TAKE
UR *grit*,
RMINATION.

courage

IN (YOU) —

and WAR

IS ALWAYS
ready,
TING.

...NEVER LET WH

DO *INTERFERE WITH*

Myle

T YOU CANNOT

WHAT YOU CAN DO.

unroe

EITHER I WILL FIND A WAY, OR I WILL MAKE ONE.

Latin Proverb

YOUR VOICE

TO BE heard.

HERE TO

IS HERE
YOU ARE
BE seen.

ONE OF THE MOST
COURAGEOUS THINGS
YOU CAN DO IS IDENTIFY
YOURSELF, KNOW WHO
YOU ARE, WHAT YOU
BELIEVE IN AND WHERE
YOU WANT TO GO.

Sheila Murray Bethel

TRUST YOURS

YOURSELF. ACT FOR

FOR YOURSELF

Marv

LF. THINK FOR

YOURSELF. SPEAK

BE YOURSELF.

ollins

DOUBT WORTH.

NEVE

INNER *st*

NEVER DOUBT YOUR OWN STRENGTH.

LIVE DARINGLY, BOLDLY, FEARLESSLY.

Henry J. Kaiser

YOU DO NOT

STRONG FOR

strong for

THE REST WILL FALL

NEED TO BE OTHERS. When you're *yourself*, INTO PLACE.

IMPOSSIBLE IS JUST AN OPINION.

Unknown

Yes, THE

ARE
REAL. But

AND YOUR HEART

CHALLENGES
YOU ARE HERE,
IS ready.

KNOW THAT THERE IS

YOU THAT IS GREATER

Christia

SOMETHING INSIDE

THAN ANY OBSTACLE.

. Larson

THERE IS NOTHING WE CANNOT LIVE DOWN, AND RISE ABOVE, AND OVERCOME.

Ella Wheeler Wilcox

Believe IN
YOU ARE. AND
YOU WI

EVERYTHING

everything

LL BE.

I AM NOT
AFRAID...
I WAS BORN
TO DO THIS.

Joan of Arc

WITH SPECIAL THANKS TO
THE ENTIRE COMPENDIUM FAMILY.

Written & Compiled by: Amelia Riedler
Designed by: Emily Carlson
Edited by: Kristin Eade

Library of Congress Control Number: 2017943797
ISBN: 978-1-943200-94-8

1st printing. Printed in China with soy inks.

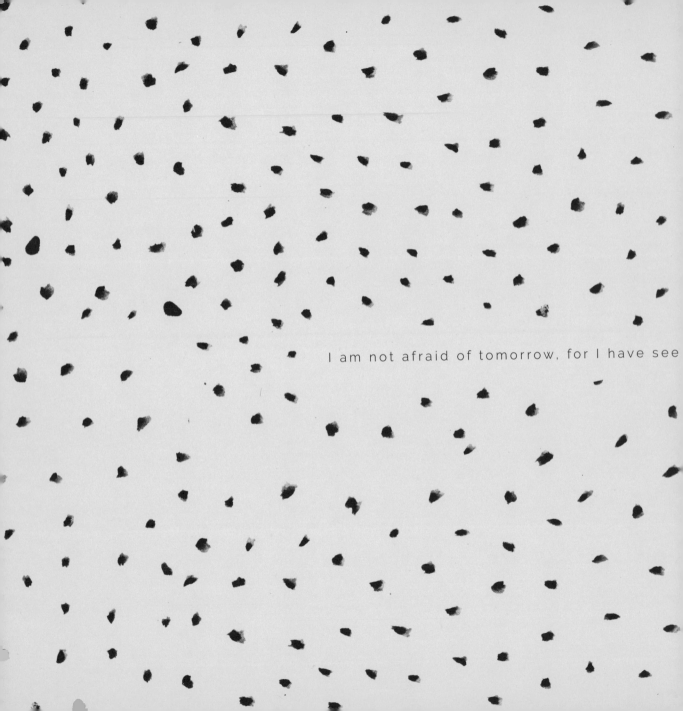

I am not afraid of tomorrow, for I have see